A Forlorn Hope

A Forlorn Hope

Third Parties
and American Political Ideology

Eric Leif Davin

DavinBooks
Box 90087
Pittsburgh, PA 15224

For Those Who Still Try

Contents

Introduction

Part I: Third Parties
The Progressive Movement of 1924
The Labor Party Movement of the 1930s
The Progressive Party, 1948
The People's Party, 1971-1978
The California Peace and Freedom Party
The Vermont Progressive Party
Why the Two-Party System Endures

Part II: American Political Ideology
The Legacy of Liberal Republicanism
Populism: America's Ideology

Introduction

Throughout American political history there have been hundreds of "third parties," so-called because they were launched in order to challenge the enduring two-party system of American politics. Except for one, all of them turned out to be dismal failures. That one exception, the Republican Party, came into existence in the 1850s when the existing party system was collapsing and one of the two main parties, the Whig Party, was disintegrating. The Republican Party was able to fill the political vacuum the Whig Party's disintegration created, and thus became one of the subsequent two dominant parties. In the absence of the disintegration of one of the two major political parties since the 1850s, none of the myriad other third parties have been able to grow into major party status.

And yet, hope springs eternal, and despite a record of almost unbroken failure, hopeful third party advocates continue to launch their parties.

In this book I will examine the rise and fall of a handful of progressive and leftist third party efforts over the last century, from the 1920s to the present, which I deem significant. The two most successful third parties in our history, other than the Republican Party, were the People's (Populist) Party of the 1890s and the Socialist Party of the early twentieth century. To discuss their political arc would require entire books, and, indeed, many books have been written on both parties attempting to explain why they ultimately failed. I will not venture into that well-trodden territory. Nevertheless, I hope the history of the more recent third parties I have chosen to discuss will prove illuminating.

After looking at the trajectories of my selected third parties, I will then explore the enduring features of the American political system, including why the two-party system has continued to dominate American politics, despite the hundreds of attempts to challenge its dominance. I will end with a discussion of the ideology of Lockian republican-populism, the foundational ideology of American politics.

Part I:
Third Parties

The Progressive Movement of 1924

Progressivism was a liberal middle class reform movement of the early twentieth century that emphasized professionalism and efficiency in municipal government and such national reforms as a graduated income tax and the direct election of U. S. Senators. It operated at the municipal, state, and national levels, manifested itself in both major political parties, as well as in independent political movements, and spread into such non-political fields as education, conservation, and social work.

In 1912 former Republican President Theodore Roosevelt, having failed at gaining the Republican presidential nomination that year, led an essentially middle class third party reform campaign as the candidate of the Progressive Party. In 1924, however, former Republican Wisconsin Governor and U. S. Senator Robert M. La Follette, who led Progressive forces in the Senate, launched an independent presidential campaign under the Progressive label that was based much more on a farmer and organized labor foundation. That campaign was not only the high water mark for independent working class political action, but, in both its base and agenda, was also a precursor of the liberal New Deal of

Democratic President Franklin D. Roosevelt a decade later.

In 1924 Robert La Follette tried, and failed, to gain that year's Republican presidential nomination, losing it to incumbent President Calvin Coolidge. In response, La Follette announced that he would run for the presidency as an independent. Various labor organizations, such as the Railroad Brotherhoods, the Amalgamated Clothing Workers, and local federations of labor, as well as progressive groups and leftist parties, such as the Socialist Party and the Chicago Farmer-Labor Party, had previously united in a broad coalition called the Conference for Progressive Political Action (CPPA). This coalition was an effort to unite all dissident groups in the country, excepting the Communists. The CPPA immediately endorsed La Follette as its presidential candidate, a nomination La Follette accepted.

Some constituent elements of the CPPA, such as the already declining Socialist Party, hoped that the CPPA and La Follette's campaign would lead to the formation of a broadly based labor party. For this reason, the Socialist Party declined to run its own presidential candidate that year and endorsed La Follette, who appeared on the ballot in Nevada and California only as the Socialist Party candidate and in Pennsylvania only as the "Socialist-Labor" candidate.

Neither the CPPA nor La Follette, however, was interested in launching a labor or third party. La Follette, for one, had a strong distaste for third party efforts and had, in fact, strongly opposed Roosevelt's Progressive Party campaign in 1912. Thus, the CPPA never transformed itself into an official political party. For this reason, except for Montana Senator Burton K. Wheeler, whom La Follette chose as his vice presidential running mate, neither it nor La Follette named any other political candidates for any offices as part of his campaign. Based upon this disavowal of third party intentions, the Executive Committee of the American Federation of Labor broke from its long tradition of political non-partisanship and gave its endorsement to La Follette's candidacy.

Republican Calvin Coolidge won the subsequent election, with 54.1% of the vote. Meanwhile, the Democratic candidate, Wall Street lawyer and J. P. Morgan partner John W. Davis, garnered 28.8% of the vote, the worst showing to this day for a Democratic Party presidential candidate. Robert La Follette, however, made the best showing to this day for an explicitly labor- and leftist-backed presidential candidate, taking 16.6% of the vote and the 13 Electoral College votes of his home state of Wisconsin. In a further eleven states, including California, where he was listed only as the Socialist Party's candidate, he ran second to Coolidge, winning more than four times the number of votes won by Davis, and almost won a majority in San Francisco. In Cleveland, he did win a majority.

In the 1950s, Samuel Lubell denied that La Follette's showing was any marker of liberal strength. Despite the fact that there were no exit polls of voter opinion at the time, he stated that, "Much of that vote, representing approval of La Follette's opposition to the war with Germany, actually had nothing to do with liberalism (Lubell, 1952, 140)." Richard Hofstadter agreed, saying, "Much of [La Follette's] support was an ethnic vote based upon his reputation as an opponent of the war; much of it, also, came from disgruntled farmers who resented their exclusion from the general prosperity (Hofstadter, 1955, 283)."

More recent evaluations of La Follette's support have disputed this claim. Thus, Andrew Strouthous (2000) argued that, since La Follette ran as an individual without a party, and so had no party organization outside of Wisconsin, he had to rely on local unions, which were major contributors of both campaign workers and funds. The Chicago Federation of Labor, for example, not only endorsed him, but also donated to his campaign, helping him win 17.9% of the Chicago vote. The Teamsters, the building trades, the Amalgamated Clothing Workers, and the International Ladies Garment Workers Union all endorsed La Follette and worked hard for him. All of the needle trades in New York City, for example, endorsed him and played a central role in the campaign, helping him win 20% of that city's vote. In Washington state, both the state Federation of Labor and the Seattle Central Labor Union endorsed La Follette. There he won 36% of the Seattle vote, twice his national average and four times what the Democrat won, and came in second in the state.

Bruce Stave (1970) noted that in Pennsylvania, where he was listed on the ballot only as the "Socialist-Labor" candidate, La Follette also won 36% of the vote in Pittsburgh. In addition, much of La Follette's campaign personnel in Pittsburgh came from the local labor movement. As one example, on Pittsburgh's South Side, densely populated by steelworkers in the local Jones and Laughlin steel plant who voted overwhelmingly for La Follette, the head of his campaign was Thomas J. Gallagher, a popular Irish-Catholic leader of the Flint Glass Workers Union. (Gallagher went on to be elected as a State Representative in 1932 and was elected to the Pittsburgh City Council in 1933.)

Further, notes Stave, A ward-level comparison of La Follette's Pittsburgh vote with Franklin D. Roosevelt's 1932 Pittsburgh vote reveals not only that La Follette's support came from the lower economic classes, but also that both La Follette and Roosevelt drew their support from much the same wards. Additionally, the wards which supported Roosevelt in 1932 and La Follette in 1924 were the very same wards which had supported Socialist Eugene V. Debs in 1912,

"[I]ndicating a firm connection between the support for the Progressive candidate in 1924 and the Socialist standard bearer of a dozen years earlier (Stave, 171)." In other words, the working class Debs-La Follette vote became the Roosevelt vote.

Noting that Al Smith, the losing Democratic presidential candidate of 1928, carried all 12 of the nation's largest cities that year, Samuel Lubell said this indicated that the nation's urban working class was already shifting toward the Democrats by the late Twenties. Thus, he said, there had been an Al Smith revolution before there was a Roosevelt revolution. One could also say that La Follette's 1924 campaign showed that there had been a La Follette revolution among the nation's urban working class before the Al Smith revolution.

Further Reading

Hofstadter, Richard, 1955, *The Age of Reform, From Bryan to F. D .R.*, New York: Vintage Books.

Lubell, Samuel, 1952, 1965, *The Future of American Politics,* Third Edition, Revised, New York: Harper & Row.

MacKay, Kenneth Campbell, 1947, *The Progressive Movement of 1924,* New York: Columbia University Press.

Stave, Bruce M., 1970, *The New Deal and the Last Hurrah, Pittsburgh Machine Politics,* Pittsburgh: University of Pittsburgh Press.

Strouthous, Andrew, 2000, *U. S. Labor and Political Action, 1918-24,* New York: St. Martin's Press.

The Labor Party Movement
of the 1930s

The standard political accounts of the labor movement of the 1930s emphasize labor's swing from a nonpartisan stance to support of President Franklin D. Roosevelt and the Democratic Party in exchange for pro-labor legislation. Forgotten is the fact that a major section of organized labor attempted – for the last time in American history – to forge a labor party in at that time. Built on the innumerable local labor party campaigns of 1932-1936, which sprang spontaneously and simultaneously into existence and groped toward national coordination, the movement suggests that the loyalty of organized labor could by no means be taken for granted by Roosevelt and the Democrats, even as late as the summer of 1936.

All told, a remarkable number of independent labor and farmer-labor parties sprang up between the years 1932 and 1936. The list of towns where such groups fielded their own candidates for local office includes Cambridge, New Bedford, and Springfield, Massachusetts; Berlin and Lincoln, New Hampshire; Danbury and Hartford, Connecticut; Buffalo and New York City, New York; Allentown, Philadelphia, and the Beaver Valley of Pennsylvania; Akron, Canton, and Toledo, Ohio; Detroit, Hamtramck, and Port Huron, Michigan; Chicago and Hillsboro, Illinois; Sioux Falls, South Dakota; Everett and Goldbar, Washington; and San Francisco, California.

Moreover, in at least ten other communities central labor unions endorsed the idea of a labor party, as did the state Federations of Labor of Rhode Island, Connecticut, Vermont, New Jersey, and Wisconsin.

In Berlin, New Hampshire, a strong local Farmer-Labor Party based in the French-Canadian pulp workers elected a mayor and majority of the city council and dominated that industrial town into the 1950s.

Over 150 union locals in Connecticut endorsed the formation of a labor party, as did the Maine Textile Council and two top Federation of Labor officials in Maine.

In Indiana the Gibson County Central Labor Union, the first labor body in the state to endorse the movement, won the support of nine locals and the Kokomo Central Labor Union for the formation of a local labor party.

In 1935, fourteen trade unions and farm organizations in South Dakota founded a state Farmer-Labor Party.

Theatrical troupes from the Brookwood Labor College, the foremost labor educational institution of the time, toured industrial centers performing plays that promoted the creation of an independent labor party.

National unions, such as the United Textile Workers, the Brotherhood of Sleeping Car Porters, and the American Newspaper Guild endorsed the formation of an independent labor party, as did the Southern Tenant Farmers Union.

At the 1935 convention of the American Federation of Labor – the convention at which the Congress of Industrial Organizations (CIO) was born – no less than thirteen national unions submitted proposals for the endorsement of a labor party. The CIO unions sought to organize workers on an industrial basis – challenging traditional notions of craft unionism that were then prevalent in AFL unions. Indeed, the labor party resolution almost passed, with a vote of 104 (including a majority of delegates representing central labor unions and state federations of labor) to 108 against the resolution.

Labor moved toward independent politics in the early 1930s after states intervened to smash strikes. What energized the creation of local labor parties from coast to coast were the great strike wave of 1934, and the repression of that strike wave. There were 1,856 strikes and over 1,470,000 workers on strike in 1934. These strikes included a big Auto-Lite strike in Toledo, a violent teamster strike in Minneapolis, a general strike in San Francisco, national strikes in auto and steel, and a strike of 400,000 textile workers in New England and the South, which was the largest single industrial conflict in the history of American organized labor.

Democratic governors in New England and the South crushed the textile workers' strike, which taught mill workers to distrust the Democratic Party. The same thing happened to workers across the country. As a result, every major center of industrial unrest in 1934, from Toledo to San Francisco, witnessed labor party activity in 1935.

The young workers in auto, rubber, textiles, and steel who poured into the CIO, which was organizing them into unions for the first time, were the same people who were demanding a labor party. This was seen as a serious problem for many in the CIO leadership. John L. Lewis (head of the Mine Workers), Sidney Hillman (head of the Clothing Workers), David Dubinsky (head of the Ladies' Garment Workers Union), and other top CIO leaders wanted to align the labor movement with Roosevelt and the Democrats. With reactionaries ganging up on Roosevelt, they felt labor could not afford to let him lose.

The vehicle they developed for combating the labor party promoters within their unions and swinging them behind Roosevelt was Labor's Non-Partisan League. The League leadership held out the possibility that this was the long-awaited move toward an independent labor party, for which many of the rank and file had been clamoring. Instead, it was a device for lining up recalcitrant labor votes for Roosevelt by defeating labor party sentiment in the CIO and in the labor movement as a whole, and wedding labor to the Democratic Party.

In this they were successful. In union after union, Non-Partisan League leadership turned back labor party sentiment to obtain endorsement of Roosevelt in 1936. The victorious CIO leadership finally signed the death certificate of their labor party rivals in their constituent unions at the first official convention of the CIO in Pittsburgh in 1938. There, with the exception of New York's American Labor Party, the CIO mandated that all future political activity was henceforth to take place within the established two-party system.

The labor party movement of the 1930s was the last time that significant elements in organized labor struggled hopefully to create an independent national labor party. Since the great realignment election of 1936, organized labor has been married, albeit somewhat shakily, to the Democratic Party.

Further Reading

Davin, Eric Leif, "The Very Last Hurrah: The Defeat of the Labor Party Idea, 1934-1936," in *We Are All Leaders: The Alternative Unionism of the Early 1930s*, ed. Staughton Lynd, Urbana: University of Illinois Press, 1996.

Davin, Eric Leif, and Staughton Lynd, "Picket Line and Ballot Box: The Forgotten Legacy of the Labor Party Movement, 1932-1936," *Radical History Review* 22 (Winter, 1979-80): 43-63.

The Progressive Party, 1948

Former Vice President Henry A. Wallace's Progressive Party presidential campaign of 1948 not only greatly diminished Communist Party influence in the organized labor movement, it also eliminated dissent over American foreign policy for a generation.

During the 1930s Henry Wallace served as President Franklin D. Roosevelt's popular and effective Secretary of Agriculture. In 1940 Roosevelt chose Wallace as his vice president and, during World War II, Wallace came to be seen as second only to Roosevelt himself as the embodiment of the New Deal. This, however, generated antagonism toward Wallace among conservative southern Democrats crucial to Roosevelt's agenda. In 1944, as Roosevelt prepared to run for an unprecedented fourth term as president, southern opposition within the Democratic Party to Wallace forced Roosevelt to choose Missouri U. S. Senator Harry S. Truman as his running mate over Wallace. As a consolation, Roosevelt appointed Wallace his Secretary of Commerce.

Then, shortly after his fourth term victory, Roosevelt died in early 1945 and Truman became president. To many, however, Truman was not seen as committed to Roosevelt's New Deal agenda as had been Roosevelt himself. Further, Truman seemed to be taking a confrontational stance toward the Soviet Union in the post-war settlement that some holdover New Dealers in the Cabinet resisted. This led to resignations until, by late 1946, Henry Wallace remained as the last New Deal veteran in Truman's Cabinet.

Meanwhile, Sidney Hillman, leader of the Amalgamated Clothing Workers union and head of the Congress of Industrial Organization's Political Action Committee (CIO-PAC), formed the National Citizen's Political Action Committee (NCPAC) in an effort to reach out beyond the labor movement to liberal groups. In September, 1946, Wallace, who was also resistant to Truman's evolving attitude toward the Soviet Union, delivered a speech before a convention of the NCPAC which departed sharply from Truman's position. In Wallace's speech he decried a "get tough" stance toward the Soviet Union, as this would only lead to increasing tensions as the Soviets responded with a "get tougher" position. Instead, he called for peaceful co-existence with the Soviet Union.

Wallace's speech angered Secretary of State James Byrnes, who was then negotiating with the Soviets in Paris over the post-war European settlement. Byrnes presented President Truman with an ultimatum: Either fire Wallace from the Cabinet, or accept his own resignation. Truman fired Wallace.

What next resulted was an intense two-year debate over the future of American relations with the Soviet Union: would there be the peaceful co-existence that Wallace advocated, or the anti-communist Cold War against the Soviets that seemed to be developing?

This debate escalated in March, 1947, when President Truman spoke before a joint session of Congress requesting military aid for Turkey and Greece, the latter of which was engaged in a fierce civil war between communist and non-communist factions. This speech was the debut of what came to be called the "Truman Doctrine," which advocated containment of the perceived global expansion of Soviet influence. In it Truman introduced the "domino theory," which came to dominate foreign policy thinking until the 1970s. If Greece fell to communist control, Truman said, then Turkey would be threatened. And if Turkey fell, the Middle East would soon follow. Western Europe would next be threatened and, thereafter, so would the United States. Soviet influence, therefore, had to be opposed from the onset, anywhere it appeared in the world.

In the winter of 1946-47, the NCPAC changed its name to the Progressive Citizens of America (PCA) and declared that it would form a third party to challenge Truman in 1948. In late December, 1947, Wallace announced that he would challenge Truman for the presidency on a program of "positive peace" with the Soviet

Union. The PCA immediately nominated him as its candidate and changed its name to the Progressive Party. In January, 1948, the Communist Party also threw its support behind Wallace's third party candidacy, as did the communist-influenced American Labor Party (ALP), which was strong in New York City.

The resulting campaign was complicated by Truman calling for making lynching and racial segregation federal crimes, his ending of racial segregation in the military via Executive Order, and the Democratic Party issuing a strong civil rights platform at its 1948 convention. This prompted southern Democrats to bolt the party and create their own third party, the Southern Democratic Party, soon dubbed the "Dixicrats." They nominated South Carolina Governor Strom Thurmond for the presidency and confidently expected that their campaign would help defeat Truman that November. This would show that the Democratic Party could not win without white southern support. Along with Wallace's Progressive Party campaign, which some predicted could win as many as five million votes, Truman appeared doomed and the Republican candidate, Thomas Dewey, was widely expected to win the presidency.

That, however, proved not to be the case. The Dixiecrats won the Electoral College votes of four Deep South states, but they did not prove crucial to the Democratic vote. Nor did Wallace's Progressive Party campaign prove to be much of a threat. Both the American Federation of Labor (AFL) and the Congress of Industrial Organizations (CIO) remained loyal to the Democratic Party, as did their working class constituencies. In addition, Wallace garnered little liberal support. Both *The Nation* and *The New Republic*, the leading liberal magazines, endorsed Truman.

Thus, Wallace only won just over one million votes, 2.3% of the total, and no Electoral College votes. Indeed, he won only 30 precincts in the entire nation, 18 of them in New York City. Eight of those 18 precincts were in the East Harlem district of American Labor Party Congressman Vito Marcantonio, and another two were in Bronx districts where the ALP was strong.

Henry Wallace's quixotic third party crusade, widely perceived to be communist dominated, as they provided much of the funding and personnel, greatly diminished Communist Party influence within the labor movement, which had remained loyal to the Democratic Party. In addition, it eliminated serious debate over American foreign policy for the next twenty-five years. A bipartisan anticommunist "coalition of the whole" henceforth dominated American attitudes toward the Soviet Union. Not until the rise of the New Left in the late 1960s with its opposition to the Vietnam War would there be a serious challenge to America's bipartisan anti-communism in foreign affairs.

Further Reading

Cantor, Milton, 1978, *The Divided Left: American Radicalism, 1900-1975*, New York: Hill and Wang.

Markowitz, Norman D., 1973, *The Rise and Fall of the People's Century: Henry A. Wallace and American Liberalism, 1941-1948*, New York: Free Press.

O'Neill, William L., 1982, *A Better World, The Great Schism: Stalinism and the American Intellectuals*, New York: Simon & Schuster.

Schmidt, Karl M., 1960, *Henry A. Wallace: Quixotic Crusade, 1948*, Syracuse: Syracuse University Press.

White, Graham, and John Maze, 1995, *Henry A. Wallace: His Search for a New World Order*, Chapel Hill: University of North Carolina Press.

The People's Party, 1971-1978

In the late 1960s and early 1970s a myriad of local radical parties sprang up all across the country in opposition to the Vietnam War and the domestic policies of the two major parties. These local third parties – all of which viewed the Democratic Party as unsalvageable – moved beyond protest to organize for the political defeat of the government.

In this sense, they were marginal to the main thrust of the social movements of the 1960s. For whatever reason, the dissident politics of the 1960s was primarily that of anti-institutional protest. As such, it emphasized demonstrations, rallies, marches, and other forms of non-party politics based on short-term mass mobilizations to present lists of "demands" to government Because it was based on such ad hoc mass mobilizations, no institutions of oppositional power that were created in the 1960s continued into future decades, unlike other decades, such as the 1930s, from which strong labor unions emerged.

The exceptions to this anti-institutional bias of 1960s protest movements were the many local radical political parties around the country, which sought permanent political power. Most of these local radical parties were loosely allied under the national umbrella of the People's Party, which ran Dr. Benjamin Spock for president in 1972 and for vice president in 1976. The California Peace and Freedom Party issued the call for the establishment of a national third party – the People's Party – in 1971.

The California Peace and Freedom Party was organized in 1967 by civil rights and anti-war activists and chose Black Panther leader Eldridge Cleaver as its presidential candidate in 1968. Not only did Cleaver appear on the ballot in California, but efforts by itinerant California organizers also managed to get him on the ballot in twenty other states.

As the 1972 presidential election drew near, however, such "colonizing" was not needed, as a large number of similar third parties had appeared in other states. As it had four years earlier, the Peace and Freedom Party sought a national non-sectarian Left presence in the upcoming election and so invited other state and local parties to join it in a nationwide coalition of like-minded parties.

Thirty-five parties from twenty-five states and the District of Columbia answered the call. The most prominent, besides the Peace and Freedom Party, were the Michigan Human Rights Party, the (Washington) D.C. Statehood Party, the Arizona New Party, the Indiana Peace and Freedom Party, the Texas New Party, and the Wisconsin Alliance. Over the Fourth of July holidays in 1971, they met in Albuquerque under the auspices of the Independent New Mexican Party and voted to maintain their separate identities, but to operate at a national level as the "Coalition."

At a founding convention in Dallas that November, hosted by the Texas New Party, the Coalition became the People's Party. The platform that emerged described the party simply as, "a mass party of the left," seeking to unite all oppressed peoples.

That 1971 founding convention also nominated anti-war activist Dr. Benjamin Spock for president and Julius Hobson, a black educator active in the D.C. Statehood Party, for vice president. The rationale for nominating Spock was that, being so few in numbers, limited in funds, and unknown in most parts of the country, the People's Party could not hope to gain any recognition at all with an unknown candidate.

The allied parties were pledged to put the Spock-Hobson ticket on the ballot back in their home states. However, some important parties in the coalition balked. The Michigan Human Rights Party, for instance, decided that it would be suicide for them to put the national ticket on the ballot in Michigan. That state's electoral laws required that the top candidate of a party obtain a certain percentage of the total vote to maintain ballot status, which the Human Rights Party already had. They feared that, with the anti-war George McGovern on the ballot as the

Democratic candidate, their own candidate would not meet the requirement, and they would lose their ballot status. Nevertheless, ten affiliates did put the ticket on the ballot, and the People's Party candidates garnered 78,751 votes.

Between 1972 and 1976 the constituent state and local parties that made up the People's Party coalition began to falter, just as the movements of the 1960s began to falter. Many of the local parties ceased to exist.

The ones that survived moved further away from the amorphous populism that they, and the People's Party, originally espoused. A brochure for the Michigan Human Rights Party, for instance, clearly stated its reasoning in originally calling for a new party: "The old parties have failed. They exist for power rather than for people. We're at war. We're victims of... an unfair tax system... poverty... repression, and decay. Only a new and radical political approach can get at the root causes of these crises. The Human Rights Party is determined to take courageous action to solve these problems." By 1974 it became evident that this "courageous action" was to declare itself socialist. The Human Rights Party thus became explicitly "socialist-feminist."

In August of that year the California Peace and Freedom Party also formally adopted a socialist-feminist platform, prompting a libertarian wing to bolt. The socialist faction of the Peace and Freedom Party had also, just that

July, at a convention in Indianapolis hosted by the Indiana Peace and Freedom Party, succeeded in having the People's Party explicitly identify itself also as a "socialist-feminist" party.

For the 1976 presidential election the People's Party nominated Margaret Wright, a black parent and education activist from Los Angeles, as its presidential candidate. Ben Spock accepted the party's nomination for vice president. The ticket, presenting itself as "A Socialist Alternative," received only 48,346 votes nationally. Three thousand of those votes came from Michigan, where the Human Rights Party had finally placed the ticket on the ballot. But, as many had feared in 1972, the statewide vote total was so low that it caused the party to lose its ballot status, a blow from which the local party never recovered.

The 1976 election was the last hurrah of the People's Party. As in Michigan, many of its affiliates had withered away. By late 1977, the People's Party essentially consisted of a national office in Washington, D.C., staffed by a single person, Casey Peters; the California Peace and Freedom Party; and the New York Working People's Party, a small sectarian group that sought to capture the mantle of the People's Party.

However, the Peace and Freedom Party was not to be captured by New York City. By early 1978 the two had gone their separate ways, and the People's Party ceased to exist. Casey

Peters turned what remained of the party's records over to the Tamiment Institute at New York University and closed the national office.

Further Reading

Davin, Eric Leif. 2012. *Radicals in Power: The New Left Experience in Office*. Lanham, Maryland: Lexington Books.
Spock, Benjamin, and Mary Morgan, *Spock on Spock: A Memoir of Growing Up With the Century*, New York: Pantheon Books, 1989.

The California Peace and Freedom Party

The California Peace and Freedom Party emerged out of the peace movement of the Vietnam War era and, along with other such third parties nation-wide, represented the electoral aspect of the 1960s New Left. While it never managed to elect more than a handful of its candidates to local office, it continues today in California as a vehicle of protest against the mainstream politics of the two major parties.

As the American military effort increased in Vietnam in the mid-1960s, so, too, did domestic opposition to that effort. By 1966 this opposition reached a critical point in the San Francisco Bay communities of Berkeley and Oakland. That year the local peace movement decided to challenge the area's incumbent pro-war Democratic U.S. Representative, Jeffrey Cohelan, in the Democratic Party primary. The peace movement, going under the name of the Community for New Politics (CNP), chose Robert Scheer as its candidate. Scheer was a graduate student in economics at the University of California in Berkeley and a leader of the anti-war movement. The Scheer campaign registered over 10,000 new voters, won 45% of the vote in the East Bay Congressional district, and carried Berkeley with 54% of the vote.

Encouraged by this showing, especially in Berkeley, the CNP decided next to contest the April, 1967 municipal elections in Berkeley. The CNP backed Ron Dellums, a leader in the local black community, for the City Council. Dellums won, providing the lone leftist voice on the Council at that time. In 1970 Dellums would go on to defeat Representative Cohelan in that year's Democratic Party primary and then represent the East Bay in Congress until 1998.

Encouraged yet again by this success in the 1967 Berkeley municipal election, the CNP next decided to launch an anti-war third party to contest the 1968 presidential election in California. The CNP felt this would be a way of pressuring the Democratic Party to nominate an anti-war candidate. Thus, in June, 1967, the CNP launched the Peace and Freedom Party (PFP), first as a CNP committee, then as an entirely separate entity. The new party began a drive to register the 64,000-plus members required for it to gain ballot status. The party met this threshold by the January, 1968, deadline, and has maintained ballot status in California (except for one four-year hiatus) ever since.

The new party also forged an alliance with the Oakland-based Black Panther Party and nominated one of its leaders, Eldridge Cleaver, as its presidential candidate in that year's election.

The PFP then sent missionaries into other states to put Cleaver on the ballot elsewhere. They were successful in doing so in 19 states. Eldridge Cleaver eventually received 36,613 votes nationally in the 1968 presidential election, about 0.02% of the total, with 75% of those votes coming from California.

As the next presidential election drew near, the PFP again sought a non-sectarian Left presence in the election. In 1971 it therefore issued a call for New Left third parties in other states to join it in a nationwide coalition. Thirty-five such parties from 25 states and the District of Columbia answered the call, resulting in the creation of the People's Party. That People's Party coalition then ran pediatrician and anti-war activist Dr. Benjamin Spock for president in 1972. In California he appeared on the ballot as the PFP candidate. Dr. Spock received 78,751 votes nationally, with 70% of them coming from California. In 1976 the People's Party ran black union activist Margaret Wright as its presidential candidate. Again, she appeared as the PFP candidate on the California ballot, where she received 85% of her national vote total.

After 1976, as the constituent state parties in the coalition collapsed, the People's Party faded away. However, the Peace and Freedom Party continued on in California, buoyed by its most valuable asset, its ballot status. Over the subsequent decades this ballot status provided a presence in California to various independent and third party presidential candidates. In 1984 the PFP put Citizens' Party presidential candidate Sonia Johnson on the California ballot. In 1988 the PFP endorsed Lenora Fulani of the New Alliance Party. In 1992 its presidential candidate was Ron Daniels, director of Jesse Jackson's 1988 campaign for the Democratic presidential nomination. In 2008 the PFP put former Green Party presidential candidate Ralph Nader on the ballot as its presidential candidate.

And so it has continued to the present. The California Peace and Freedom Party, the last direct remnant of the myriad New Left third parties of the Vietnam War era, still provides ballot status in the nation's largest state to dissident independent and third party presidential candidates. So long as it retains its ballot status, the Peace and Freedom Party will probably continue doing so into the foreseeable future.

Further Reading

Chester, Lewis; Godfrey Hodson; and Bruce Page. 1969. *An American Melodrama: The Presidential Campaign of 1968.* London: Deutsch.

Davin, Eric Leif. 2012. *Radicals in Power: The New Left Experience in Office.* Lanham, Maryland: Lexington Books.

English, David. 1969. *Divided They Stand.* New York: Prentice Hall.

Lang, Serge. 1967. *The Scheer Campaign.* New York: W. A. Benjamin.

Rorabaugh, W. J. 1989. *Berkeley at War: The 1960s.* New York: Oxford University Press.

The Vermont Progressive Party

The Vermont Progressive Party is a competitive third party that currently provides a visible democratic socialist presence in the Green Mountain State's politics. Its birth and success, however, cannot be separated from the rise of independent socialist Bernie Sanders to represent Vermont in the United States Senate.

Bernie Sanders moved to Burlington, Vermont, from his native Brooklyn, New York, in 1970. Burlington had a population of only 38,000, with the Greater Burlington Metropolitan Area totaling 133,000. With 66% of Vermont's 500,000 statewide population living in rural areas, Vermont was the most rural state in the nation.

Vermont had been rock solid Republican since the Civil War. Even President Franklin D. Roosevelt failed to carry it in his 1936 landslide when he won every state in the Union except for Maine and Vermont. Indeed, no Democratic presidential candidate won the state until Lyndon Johnson did so in his 1964 landslide. That feat, however, was not to be repeated again until Bill Clinton won the state in 1992. It was not until 1962 that Vermont elected its first Democratic governor.

Nevertheless, change was coming to Vermont in the late 1960s, as the "back to the land" ethos of the time encouraged many young people to migrate to the state. As demographics changed, so too did the state's politics. In 1970, perhaps two dozen New Left activists launched the Liberty Union, one of the myriad New Left third parties that sprang up nation-wide at that time. The Liberty Union focused on statewide elections, contesting, and losing, every statewide election in the 1970s.

In 1972 it affiliated with the national People's Party coalition and placed that party's presidential candidate, Dr. Benjamin Spock, on the Vermont ballot. He won only 1,010 votes in the state. In 1976 the Liberty Union failed to place the People's Party's presidential candidate, Margaret Wright, on the ballot. However, in 1980 it was able to place David McReynolds, the Socialist Party's presidential nominee, on the ballot as the Liberty Union candidate. McReynolds garnered only 136 Vermont votes for president. Such dismal showings frustrated many Liberty Union activists, such as Bernie Sanders.

Bernie Sanders wandered into his first Liberty Union meeting in 1971, and wandered out as its 1972 candidate in a special January election for the U. S. Senate. He received about 2% of the vote in the subsequent election. In 1972 Sanders also ran that November as the Liberty Union's candidate for governor. The

Liberty Union again ran him for the Senate in 1974 and again for governor in 1976.

In 1977 Sanders resigned from the Liberty Union, complaining of its lack of interest in local elections. He had noticed that, while he had never received more than 6% of the vote in any of the state-wide elections, he'd won as high as 15% of the vote in Burlington, and an even higher percentage in some of the town's wards. He decided to concentrate all his resources on a run for local office in Burlington.

While Republicans dominated Vermont's state politics, Democrats had long dominated Burlington. Indeed, Democratic dominance was so strong that Republicans had ceased running candidates for mayor. Thus, in 1981, when long-time Democratic Mayor Gordon Paquette came up for re-election, he faced no Republican opponent. Sanders decided to run against him as an independent socialist. Against all expectations, Sanders won by ten votes. A Citizens' Party candidate, Terry Bouricius, also won election to the 13-member Board of Aldermen.

The stunned Democrats and Republicans on the Board of Aldermen united to stymie the agenda of Bernie Sanders at every point, even denying him approval of his appointments to various city offices. In 1982, in response, Sanders backed a slate of Aldermen candidates against the seven Democrats then up for re-election. Four of his candidates, including two members of the Citizens' Party, won the election. In 1983

Sanders faced both Democratic and Republican opponents for the mayoralty, but he won his first re-election with 52% of the vote. The Sanders coalition next picked up a sixth Alderman seat in the 1984 election. By then only two Democrats remained on the Board of Aldermen they had long dominated, with five Republicans filling the remaining seats. In 1985 Sanders was re-elected yet again, with 55.3% of the vote. In 1987 the Republicans declined to run a mayoralty candidate, and Sanders beat his sole Democratic opponent with 55.6% of the vote.

In 1989 Sanders announced that he would not run for re-election, and his allies on the Board of Aldermen were faced with a post-Sanders crises. Would the political change in Burlington survive without him? They decided to find out. Calling themselves the "Progressive Coalition," they nominated Peter Clavelle, Burlington's director of economic and community development, for the mayoralty. Clavelle defeated his sole opponent, a Democrat, with 54% of the vote. The Progressive Coalition re-elected Clavelle as mayor in 1991. Although defeated in 1993, the Progressive Coalition returned Clavelle to the mayor's office in 1995, where he remained without a break until leaving office in 2006. Progressive Bob Kiss, who had served as a Progressive in the Vermont State House since 2001, replaced him. Like his predecessors, Bob Kiss would be re-elected the Progressive Mayor of Burlington again and again. In 2012 he announced he would not run for re-election and, for the first time in 31 years, a Democrat won election to the mayor's office.

Meanwhile, in 1990 Bernie Sanders decided to challenge incumbent Republican Peter Smith for Vermont's sole seat in the U. S. House of Representatives. The Democrats failed to name a strong candidate for the race and Sanders, running as an independent socialist, won 13 of Vermont's 14 counties that November, defeating the Republican by 56% to 40%, with the Democrat winning 3% of the vote. In 1992 Sanders won re-election to Congress with 58% of the vote to 31% for the Republican and 8% for the Democrat. Sanders won every House race thereafter, with the Democrats not even fielding a candidate in 1994. In his last House campaign in 2004, Sanders won 67% of the vote against 24% for the Republican and 7% for the Democrat.

In 2006 one of Vermont's U. S. Senate seats became vacant and Sanders ran for it. He easily won the Democratic primary, but declined the nomination to run as an independent socialist in the November general election. Sanders easily beat the Republican candidate with 65% of the vote, sweeping every county in Vermont and almost every city and town. Sanders thus became the U. S. Senate's only independent socialist, which, although he caucuses with the Democrats, he remains to this day. He easily won re-election to the Senate in 2012 and in 2016 almost won the Democratic Party's presidential nomination. In

2018, without even campaigning, he once more won Vermont's Democratic Party primary for the Senate, but declined it again in order to seek re-election to the Senate as an independent.

Even as Sanders moved on to Congress in 1990, Burlington's Progressive Coalition also won state-wide office that year. Two of Burlington's Progressive Aldermen, including Terry Bouricius, who was originally elected with Sanders in 1981, won election to the Vermont State House of Representatives. Terry Bouricius served in the House until 2001. He then retired, after serving for 20 years without a break as a Progressive office holder. Since 1990 the Progressives have elected people to office in a number of other Vermont towns and have remained a force on the Burlington Board of Selectmen, holding four seats as of 2018. They have also continually elected candidates to both the Vermont State House and the State Senate. In 2018, seven Progressives were in the State House and three in the State Senate. In addition, the Vermont Lt. Governor was a Progressive.

In 1999 the Progressive Coalition changed its name to the "Progressive Party." As such it continues to champion democratic socialism in what was once a solidly Republican state, but which has since become the only seriously competitive three-party state in the nation.

Further Reading

Davin, Eric Leif. 2012. *Radicals in Power: The New Left Experience in Office*. Lanham, Maryland: Lexington Books.

Guma, Greg. 1989. *The People's Republic: Vermont and the Sanders Revolution*. Shelburne, VT: New England Press.

Rice, Tom. (Summer, 1985.) "Who Votes for a Socialist Mayor? The Case of Burlington, Vermont." *Polity 4*.

Sanders, Bernie, with Huck Gutman. 1997. *Outsider in the House*. London: Verso.

Soifer, Steven. 1991. *The Socialist Mayor*. Westport, CT: Bergin and Garvey.

Why the Two-Party System Endures

Bernie Sanders is politically astute. He understands the rules of the game. That's why he ran for president in 2016 inside the Democratic Party, despite being registered as an Independent. As Bernie said when he announced his candidacy for the Democratic presidential nomination, the hurdles for an independent campaign are virtually impossible to overcome.

Those hurdles also explain why the Green Party on the Left and the Libertarian Party on the Right, like all such third parties, will remain exercises in political futility. Despite all the furor they created in the 2016 election, and despite the fact that the candidates of the two major parties, Democrat Hillary Clinton and Republican Donald Trump, had the highest unfavorable ratings in political memory, the two minor parties performed miserably, with the Libertarian Party garnering about 3% of the vote and the Greens about 1% of the vote. Indeed, over the last century, and even before, third parties in America have faltered and failed.

Even where they have survived within a state, such as in California with the Peace and Freedom Party and in Vermont with the Progressive Party, they have not been able to expand outside of the state. Nor, given the track record of third parties, is the long-term survival of even those two parties a given.

Why has the track record of American third parties been so dismal?

The hurdles making third party activity peripheral in American politics have to do with the constitutionally imposed limitations on political representation that the politically conservative Founders wrote into the Constitution. Foremost among these limitations is the apportionment of legislative seats to single member geographic districts, and the election within those districts by a "first past the gate" winner-take-all plurality. This means that any political movement or organization that seeks to gain representation in either the U. S. House of Representatives or in state legislatures must be able to win an electoral majority within a specific geographical location. A minority showing – which any new insurgent political movement is bound to be – up to even 49.9% of the vote will yield exactly zero political representation. If a minority political movement happens to win a plurality in a three-way race, the two major parties have usually defeated the movement's candidates in the next election by running a fusion ticket against it.

Thus, anything less than a majority is pointless, and most voters are savvy enough to realize at least this much about our elections. This is why they stick with the established major parties. What happened in my own Pittsburgh precinct in the 2016 elections illustrates this. My neighborhood is an extremely progressive neighborhood and my precinct is extremely progressive. In the April, 2016, Democratic primary, Bernie Sanders crushed Hillary Clinton by 146 votes to 63 in my precinct. In the November general election, however, after Hillary Clinton had defeated Sanders for the party's nomination, those progressive Sanders voters then voted for Hillary Clinton, rather than for the Green Party's Jill Stein in some kind of futile protest, as Hillary won 365 votes in my precinct to only eight (8) votes for Jill Stein.

A minority showing across many districts is equally futile. Under a parliamentary or proportional representation system, winning five or fifteen percent of the vote would be enough for either representation in office, or at least recognition as a major player. But under our "first-past-the-post" system, such a showing garners no political power and quick oblivion. For example, in 1992 millionaire businessman Ross Perot won 19% of the presidential vote as a third party candidate. Who, today, even remembers Ross Perot?

Likewise, in 1912 the Socialist Party won six percent (6%) of the vote, but elected no one to Congress, and declined continually thereafter into oblivion. On the other hand, a six percent (6%) showing by the Labour Party in the 1910 elections in Great Britain under its parliamentary system gave it 42 seats in Parliament.

These political realities also go a long way toward explaining why the two major American parties have, for a large part, muted class appeals in the interest building a cross-class coalition of voters that will deliver the crucial 50.1% of the vote needed to win 100% of the political power. If you go too far to the Left, as with the Green Party, or too far to the Right, as with Ross Perot's party or the Libertarian Party, you will loose. Thus, you must straddle the broad middle, and bring enough voters into your Big Tent to win that winner-take-all slim majority.

This also explains the reasonable reluctance of voters to vote for a third party. Any vote for a third party must take votes away from the major party closest to the third party ideologically, thus becoming, in effect, a vote for your worst enemy. Ross Perot's 19% of the vote in 1992 came overwhelmingly from Republican voters, thus guaranteeing Democrat Bill Clinton the election, even though he won only 42% of the vote. The same thing happened again in 1996 when Ross Perot ran once again, pulling votes from the Republican candidate, thus guaranteeing Bill Clinton's re-election, even though Clinton won only 46% of the vote.

Likewise, in the 2000 presidential election, almost 100,000 Florida voters voted for Green Party candidate Ralph Nader. George W. Bush, the Republican candidate, ended up (supposedly) winning Florida by 137 votes. He thus won 100% of Florida's Electoral College votes and, therefore, the presidency. If even one percent (1,000) of Green Party voters had voted for the Democratic candidate instead, Al Gore would have won Florida in a relative landslide and been elected president.

Again, in the 2016 election, the Green Party's Jill Stein won more votes in Wisconsin and Michigan than Republican Donald Trump's exceedingly slim margin of victory over Hillary Clinton in those states. Had those Green Party voters opted for Clinton over Trump, she would have won both states. The same phenomenon happened in other states. Green Party voters thus helped put their worst enemy, Donald Trump, in the White House.

In American politics, therefore, third parties that start out small, stay small. If they can't win elections, and the obstacles to doing so are overwhelming, they will eventually fade into oblivion. Thus, America is, and will remain, a two-party system, because those are the rules of the game written into the Constitution by the Founders.

Therefore, any real hope of bringing about political change in America must begin by working within one of the existing two major parties, however flawed they may be, however difficult that may be. For progressives, that means working within the Democratic Party.

For example, in the 2018 Democratic primary election, an insurgent challenger from the Democratic Socialists of America (DSA) overwhelmed the status quo incumbent Democratic State Representative in both my precinct and in the entire district to become the new Democratic nominee. Because there was no Republican opponent in the general election, this primary victory assured her of victory in the general election.

The same thing happened in the adjacent State Representative district, where another DSA candidate unseated the incumbent in the Democratic primary. She, too, had no Republican opposition in the general election, assuring her of victory. And the same thing happened at the same time in Philadelphia with two DSA candidates unseating two other incumbent Democratic State Representatives in the 2018 primary election.

And then there is Alexandria Ocasio-Cortez, the young Democratic Socialist of America candidate in New York's Bronx U.S. House of Representatives district. In the 2018 Democratic Party primary she defeated the long-time incumbent Representative who was number four in the House Democratic leadership. Because she faced no Republican opponent in the general election, she was assured of victory, the same as the four DSA State Representatives in Pittsburgh and Philadelphia. She thus became the only avowed socialist in the House of Representatives… and she is a Democrat.

Clearly, the Democratic Socialists of America have identified a winning political strategy within America's two-party system. The key to victory for insurgent Leftists is not via the graveyard of dissident third parties. The key to victory is realizing that the American two-party system will endure, and working within that two-party system.

Part II:

American Political Ideology

The Legacy of
Liberal Republicanism

As the 2016 campaigns of Bernie Sanders and Donald Trump dramatically illustrated, the dominant ideology of political dissent in America is, and always has been, populism, the glorification of "the people" against the elites.

Populism, in turn, is grounded in the ideology of John Locke's liberal republicanism. If we want to understand the ideology that governs American politics, therefore, we should have an understanding of this political philosophy, for even if "the people" are completely unaware of the origin and details of republicanism, it is what politically motivates them, and thus determines American politics.

The ideology of republicanism has always dominated American politics and it promises certain things about the country. For example, in the Declaration of Independence of 1776, Thomas Jefferson had stated that it was a "self evident truth" that "all men are created equal and endowed by their Creator with certain inalienable rights," the chief among them being "life, liberty, and the pursuit of happiness." The "self evident" idea that all men were born free and equal was, of course, not original to Jefferson. Indeed, he acknowledged his intellectual debt to

Enlightenment thinkers who came before him, most importantly English theorist John Locke.

In his 1690 *Essay Concerning the True Original Extent and End of Civil Government,* written to justify the new constitutional monarchy established by the Glorious Revolution of 1688, Locke laid down the principles of Jefferson's Declaration. In this essay, Locke elaborated his concept of limited government based on the consent of the governed. His starting point, however, was a primitive state of nature comprised of free and equal individuals. The "law of nature," therefore, entitled all individuals equally to life, liberty, and property.

However, by a social contract they delegated the administration of this law of nature to government, while retaining the inherent rights to freedom and equality that the "law of nature" gave them. Jefferson embedded not only Locke's doctrines, but also his very phrases into the Declaration of Independence.

By doing so, however, he was simply stating what most Americans believed. The New World of America, it seemed to them, was the very embodiment of Locke's original "state of nature." Indeed, Locke himself had once written that, "In the beginning, all the world was America..." Further, beginning with the Mayflower Compact of 1620, those coming to America from Europe had traditionally written social contracts establishing a form of government agreed to by free and equal property owners.

Thus, historian Louis Hartz famously pointed out in 1955 in his *The Liberal Tradition in America,* "Locke dominates American political thought, as no thinker anywhere dominates the political thought of a nation. He is a massive national cliché." Hartz went on to note that America had never experienced feudalism, nor did it have a titled aristocracy. And, with the triumph of the Revolution, it no longer had a king, nor any serious political tendency defending monarchism. Everyone believed in the republican form of limited government based upon the consent of free individuals, and all political debate took place within that narrow range of ideas based on inherent rights to equality and property ownership. "Catastrophes have not been able to destroy" the idea, Hartz argued, "proletariats have refused to give it up." Hence, "In...the Jeffersonian and Jacksonian eras...virtually everyone, including the nascent industrial worker, has the mentality of the independent entrepreneur."

Such beliefs were based on a fair amount of reality. While America was not Thomas Jefferson's idealized yeoman Eden, an analysis of the 1798 land tax figures reveals that 52% of the free white males were farmers who owned their own land. Thus, they were economically independent and participated in political discourse as socio-economic equals at a time when property ownership was a prerequisite for being a voter. This was no doubt the highest percentage of land-owning "citizens" in the world at that time. Not only was there more equality in 1800 among free white males than anywhere else, there was also probably more equality in America for this population than there ever would be again. Further, there was the hope and expectation that landless free white males would eventually move up to become landowners themselves.

It should come as no surprise, therefore, to discover that the labor literature of the age was saturated with the idea of yeoman free holding and, "During the Jacksonian era…labor writers were clinging to Jefferson's small propertied individualism…. Jefferson emphasized the concrete fact of the ownership of property, which to be sure was not a characteristic of the industrial worker. But…liberalism…was largely a psychological matter, a product of the spirit of Locke…[that] could infect the factory as well as it infected the land."

Even in the 1830s, however, Americans were already feeling the strains and tensions resulting from the centralizing and monopolizing tendencies of a developing industrial capitalism. Their deep-rooted belief in liberal republicanism informed their attitudes toward the emerging new order. Thus, historian Herbert Gutman tells us, "workers transformed the political, social, and economic beliefs and practices they carried from the American Revolution into a distinctive critique of early American capitalism. Central to these beliefs and practices was republicanism. The transformation of American men and women into dependent wage earners in the years before 1840 tested not only their adaptability to specialized labor, but also the appropriateness of their republican ideology.... 'Give a man power over my subsistence,' Alexander Hamilton had warned, 'and he has a right to my whole moral body.' Hamilton and his generation did not live into the early industrial capitalist era, but republican ideology survived them and gained a new life among the artisans and laborers of industrializing America."

This same fundamental belief in Lockian liberalism, the belief in liberty, equality, and the inherent right to own property, was at the heart of the Free Soil movement of the 1840s and resulted in the birth of the Republican Party in the 1850s. By then, however, the generalized Lockian ideal had acquired a specific name: Free Labor. It was a concept, Eric Foner tells us in his seminal work, *Free Soil, Free Labor, Free Men,* that was "the heart of the Republican ideology, and expressed a coherent social outlook, a model of the good society... For Republicans, 'free labor' meant labor with economic choices, with the opportunity to quit the wage-earning class. A man who remained all his life dependent on wages for his livelihood appeared almost as unfree as the southern slave."

President Abraham Lincoln reflected this Lockian free labor ideal in 1861 at the beginning of the Civil War, placing that war in context. A slave was a slave forever, he said, but in the North, there was "no such...thing as a free man being fixed for life in the condition of a hired laborer.... Men, with their families...work for themselves on their farms, in their houses, and in their shops, taking the whole product for themselves, and asking no favors of capital on the one hand nor of hired laborers or slaves on the other."

Northern farmers and workers were, in this view of the ideal society, essentially economically self-sufficient middle class small businessmen or, if they were not at present, hoped soon to become so. It was this concept of an ideal society of free small property owners that lay behind the plans of some Radical Republicans after the war to break up the large antebellum southern plantations and redistribute the land to the ex-slaves. With the right to vote and "forty acres and a mule" the ex-slaves would have both democratic and economic freedom and equality, and would thus be able to defend their rights in the postbellum southern world.

In fact, Eric Foner says, "The Republicans' enmity toward the South was intimately bound up with their loyalty to the society of small-scale capitalism which they perceived in the North. It was its identification with the aspirations of the farmers, small entrepreneurs, and craftsmen of northern society that gave the Republican ideology much of its dynamic, progressive, and optimistic quality. Yet, paradoxically, at the same time of its greatest success, the seeds of a later failure of that ideology were already present. Fundamental changes were at work in the social and economic structure of the North, transforming and undermining many of its free labor assumptions." In the years after the Civil War, the ideal of social mobility continued to be widely held, but it was already becoming increasingly unlikely that an industrial worker or a farm laborer would ever achieve economic independence.

It was this conflict between old ideals and new realities that generated the endemic and increasing social conflict in the North. In this regard, David Montgomery demonstrated in his path breaking 1967 book, *Beyond Equality,* how the republican ideology of equality motivated workers' movements in the North to raise fundamental challenges to industrial capitalism during both the Civil War and the subsequent Reconstruction years. Because of their ideology, workers believed a good society was one of "haves and will-haves." And, they believed, that was what the land of equal opportunity had always promised its citizens.

Industrial capitalism, however, with its centralizing and monopolizing tendencies, challenged their traditional values of individualism, free competition, and equal opportunity, and was transforming America into a society of "haves and have-nots." They resisted this development, Montgomery argues. Indeed, Montgomery's important contribution to the discussion was the insight that the resulting class conflict, in which workers attempted to make the new and alien social order more humane and egalitarian, was a primary reason for the collapse of Radical Reconstruction. Northern labor leaders argued that, just as the South was being reconstructed to create a more egalitarian society, so must the North also be reconstructed in the same way. The increasing class conflict in the North encouraged the captains of industry and Republican politicians to entertain second thoughts about the wisdom of an egalitarian southern Reconstruction.

Recent scholars echoed Montgomery's interpretation of the Reconstruction Era. For example, in her 2001 book, *The Death of Reconstruction,* Heather Cox Richardson closely investigates postbellum newspapers, magazines, letters and speeches to persuasively argue that it was Northern class conflict, with its incessant challenges to the new industrial economy and calls for wealth redistribution, more than the virulent racism of the time, which contributed the most to the "death of Reconstruction."

And, in fact, things were changing quickly in the wake of the Civil War. At the end of the Civil War in 1865, half or more of all adult Americans were self-employed, but by 1870, according to that year's census, 70% of Americans were already directly or indirectly dependent upon wages, economically dependent, in other words, upon someone else.

To many observers it seemed that American civilization was on the brink of chaos and destruction, as the old order died and the newly emerging industrial capitalist order seemed inimical to all that people held dear. Within a short span of time they saw the United States transformed from an overwhelmingly agricultural society dominated by farmers, merchants, and small town artisans into an urban industrial society dominated by large factories, powerful corporations, and business elites. The changes challenged their ideas about the type of society America should be.

Herbert Gutman quotes Pittsburgh steel magnate Andrew Carnegie as boasting in his 1886 book, *Triumphant Democracy,* that, "The old nations of the earth creep on at a snail's pace, but the Republic thunders past with the rush of an express." But, Gutman goes on to say, "The articulate steelmaster…had missed the point. The very rapidity of the economic changes occurring in Carnegie's lifetime meant that many, unlike him, lacked the time, historically, culturally, and psychologically, to be separated or alienated from settled ways of work and life and from relatively fixed beliefs."

Thus, Gutman says, "Certain elements in the preindustrial American social structure and in older patterns of popular ideology persisted strongly into the post-Civil War urban world, profoundly affected behavior, and served as a source of recurrent opposition to the power and status of the new industrialist."

Basic to the ideas workers continued to hold into the postbellum years was, of course, the essentially middle class republican ideal of a good society. Gutman cites a coal miner speaking in 1876 who declared that, "The theory of Republicanism does not allow the laboring population to be reduced to poverty and dependence on the will of a few, and the virtual abrogation of our political rights and privileges."

Historian Melvyn Dubofsky also notes that, "Both workers and industrialists might subscribe to the importance of home ownership. But what is one to make of Carnegie's multimillion-dollar Fifth Avenue mansion compared to the two-room shack of a coal miner? Workers, as well as employers, might boast about America's democratic-republican heritage, its Exceptionalism as a real 'people's republic.' But did democratic-republicanism carry precisely the same implications for both social classes? Certainly it seems likely that workers and industrialists might draw different meanings about the realities of the American political order from the facts of industrial conflict."

And, indeed, the industrial conflict of the non-union era before the New Deal of the 1930s cannot be really understood without understanding these rival interpretations of what America was all about. The New Deal brought a resolution to this conflict by, at last, guaranteeing ordinary people a modicum of economic justice and equality in the new industrial order. However, the history of America since the 1930s has essentially been a battle of corporate champions to repeal the New Deal and its programs, such as Social Security and the protection of labor unions via such laws as the National Labor Relations Act (the Wagner Act), which governs labor-management relations to this day.

And, over the decades, the political pushback from "the people" has always been motivated by their baked-in belief in the type of egalitarian society America should be. This is a society which gives ordinary people a shot at economic security and which believes in equal rights for all, privileges for none. It is the ideology of populism, of "the people" against the elites, and it remains, as it always has been, the dominant ideology of political dissent in America. It is the language of the 99% against the 1%, of the people vs. the elites.

Successful political organizers will be aware of this indigenous political orientation and couch their arguments in its language when making their appeals.

Populism: America's Ideology

In my previous discussion of John Locke's ideas on republicanism I said that his political philosophy is the basis of populism. After Donald Trump's electoral victory in 2016, populism suffered a lot of abuse at the hands of political pundits and Sunday morning talk show hosts. A prominent critic was Fareed Zakaria, a *Washington Post* columnist and sometime essayist for *TIME*. The title of one of his attacks on populism expressed his dire view of this political ideology, "Populism on the March: Why the West is in Trouble," an essay of his that appeared in the November-December, 2016, issue of *Foreign Affairs*.

This fear and distrust of populism among the elites has a long history, going back at the very least to the 1950s, when liberal intellectuals decried the demagoguery of Senator Joseph McCarthy. What all these media commentators seemingly fail to understand with their trash talk against populism is that populism is not a strange aberration of democracy that rears its ugly head during times of crisis.

Broadly speaking, populism is the belief that the will of the people should prevail over the will of privileged elites. Thus, populism is the concept of democracy itself, and elite fears of populism are actually fears of democracy. This fear of democracy has a tradition in this country that goes back to our founding as a nation when the Founders wrote the Constitution to curtail what they saw as the dangers of too much democracy.

Nor is populism the monolithic philosophy these commentators portray. It can be manifested as what might be called "Right Populism," as exemplified by Donald Trump, and is the version of populism these pundits fear and decry. But it can also be manifested as "Left Populism," as exemplified by Bernie Sanders. Both versions are powerful. In the 2016 primaries, Donald Trump garnered 13.3 million votes with his version of Right Populism. But Bernie Sanders garnered almost as many votes, 13 million, with his version of a Left Populism that promised "A Future To Believe In," and he won 22 states, including states that Hillary Clinton lost in the general election, such as Indiana, Wisconsin, and Michigan.

Left Populism is a protest tradition, one that champions the common people against the rich and powerful, that has always been America's dominant ideology of dissent. Most American radicals, including working class radicals, have commonly thought of themselves as "the people " instead of "the workers," even though they may have been of the working class.

Given the dominance of Left Populism in American protest thought, it should surprise no one that the all-time best-selling history of American radicalism, with well over one million copies in print, celebrates America's Left Populist heritage. It is, of course, Howard Zinn's *A People's History of the United States.*

Before the radical upsurge of the 1960s, the other great period of twentieth century protest was the 1930s. Despite what the Left might wish to believe about the legendary labor upheavals of the 1930s, it was Left Populism, not some variant of Marxism, that mobilized "the workers" in that earlier period of radicalism. Indeed, the labor struggles of the Thirties were part of a wider Left Populist movement at that time for inclusion of the downtrodden in the American Dream. This is why they rallied to President Franklin D. Roosevelt and made the Democratic Party the majority party in the New Deal Era. Journalist Bill Moyers recalls that FDR seemed to be the champion of all the "Forgotten Men" who were "Lost in America," the entire dispossessed and tossed aside.

Bill Moyers was raised a Baptist in East Texas where his father had left school after the fourth grade to begin life as a cotton picker. His father bought a radio with his meager savings just so he could listen to FDR, "the aristocrat speaking up for common people," during his "Fireside Chats." And the message of FDR and his New Deal, said Moyers, the message his father heard coming over that radio in the East Texas cotton fields was this: "Class and power were not fixed by Nature; inequality was wrong and unemployment humiliating; runaway capitalism could be tamed, privilege checked, monopolies broken up, an end put to government by organized money. To people down and out, broken and feeling betrayed, Roosevelt talked of democracy. He made them think they had a stake in it and a responsibility for it."

The common people Moyers spoke of embodied a down-to-earth, blue collar, multi-ethnic, populist ideal we find elsewhere in popular culture during the Thirties. This ideal is found, for instance, in the thousands of photos taken by the photographers sent out across America by the Farm Security Administration (FSA). From 1935 to 1943 Roy Stryker directed a team of some twenty FSA photographers who produced over 270,000 pictures of America's "common people." Stryker's photographers took some of the iconic images we have of the Great Depression, such as Dorothea Lange's Okie Madonna, broken down somewhere in a California farm field with her children hanging on her.

The reason these photos are so populist is because Roy Stryker deliberately sought pictures of "the common people," the hard working survivors who built America. "I think it's significant," Stryker later said, "that in our entire collection we have only one picture of Franklin

Roosevelt, the most newsworthy man of the era -- this, mind you, in a collection that's sometimes said to have reported the feel and smell and taste of the Thirties even more vividly than the news media.... you'll find no record of big people or big events in the collection.... not a single shot of Wall Street, and absolutely no celebrities."

This ideal was in the air. In 1936, in what he termed his own favorite poem, Carl Sandburg celebrated "The People, Yes!"[i] In 1941, Pulitzer Prize-winning poet Stephen Vincent Benet urged us to "Listen To The People." These people included, "Paul Bunchick and the Greek who runs the Greek's/ The black-eyed children out of Sicily/ All of them there and all of them a nation. / Our voice is not one voice, but many voices. / Not one man's, not the greatest, but the people's."

In 1942 Aaron Copeland wrote a hymn of praise to "the common man" in his "Lincoln Portrait," the most stirring portion of which is his triumphant beginning, the "Fanfare for the Common Man." Copeland has a reader quote passages from Abraham Lincoln to the accompaniment of stirring music, passages such as "The spirit of slavery is the same as the spirit that says, 'You work and toil and earn bread, and I'll eat it.' No matter in what shape it comes, whether from a mouth of a king, or from one race of men as an apology for enslaving another race, it is the same tyrannical principle."

This was a theme also commonly expressed by radical labor unions in the Thirties, such as the Independent Textile Union of Rhode Island, which had approvingly published the very same Lincoln passage five years before in a 1937 issue of its newspaper.

But perhaps the musical genre that most closely reflected the spirit of the times was folk music. Americans have long composed and sung "traditional" songs such as cowboy laments, Delta blues, Kentucky bluegrass, and the hillbilly songs of Appalachia, with their roots in Elizabethan and Scots-Irish ballads. It was not until the twentieth century, however, that such songs came to be identified as "folk songs" of "the people," a populist musical genre that cohered in the 1930s. And it is no accident that the music we most closely identify with the Thirties is folk music, a genre which describes the lives, loves, and labors of the common people.

It is also no accident, then, that the two periods that witnessed the proliferation of folk songs, the Thirties and the Sixties, were also the only two eras of the twentieth century that witnessed the emergence and flowering of significant populist and oppositional countercultures.

Even the obdurate Communist Party eventually adopted the Left Populism of the times with its 1935 "Popular Front" strategy. That year the party changed its official slogan to,

"Communism is Twentieth Century Americanism." Meanwhile, the volunteers it sent to fight in Spain against the fascists in that country's civil war did so as members of "The Abraham Lincoln Brigade." At the same time, the Communist-affiliated Composers Collective began including in its *Workers Song Books* indigenous folk music of all types, including songs of farmers, miners, urban workers, and African-Americans – songs of "the people." It should come as no surprise, therefore, that the Communist Party reached its most influence and its highest membership levels during this Popular Front period when it promoted Left Populism.

The most influential folk singer of the Thirties was no doubt Woody Guthrie. He was born into an impoverished Oklahoma dust bowl family and was closely associated with the Communist Party. Guthrie composed more than a thousand songs reflecting the decade's spirit of Left Populist protest. Perhaps his most well known song is "This Land is Your Land," which declared, "this land belongs to you and me," not, it suggested, to the rich and the corporations.

In 1941 Guthrie joined Pete Seeger, Lee Hays, and others to form the Almanac Singers, a popular folk group that sang for C.I.O. (Congress of Industrial Organizations) organizing campaigns and political rallies. After World War II, as America became more politically conservative, Guthrie, Seeger, and other members of the Almanac Singers kept the Left

Populist spirit of folk music alive through such groups as People's Songs. It was at a meeting of the People's Songs Board of Directors that Pete Seeger and Lee Hays wrote "If I Had a Hammer," which gained widespread popularity in the early Sixties after the folk trio of Peter, Paul, and Mary made it a hit. In the song, Seeger and Hays proclaimed that they would hammer out justice and freedom "all over this land."

This Left Populist theme was also echoed in the films of Italian director Frank Capra, perhaps the most popular and successful film director of the 1930s, responsible for such films as "Mr. Smith Goes To Washington" and "Meet John Doe". Born in Sicily in 1897, Capra immigrated to Los Angeles with his parents in 1903. When America entered World War I, he joined the army. After the Armistice, Capra returned to Los Angeles, but was unable to find a job. He bummed around for several years, working at odd jobs, ending up down and out in San Francisco. It was during those days that Capra came to believe that, "The rich have it all, but accomplish little." The essence of Frank Capra's Left Populism, reflected in his subsequent films, was that it was the decent, hard-working, "little guy" who really represented all that was most American -- while the wealthy and the representatives of the powerful represented a venal corruption of the American ideal.

This struggle for more democracy – for more government of the people, by the people, and for the people, in the words of Abraham Lincoln at Gettysburg – is, and always has been, the central conflict of American politics. Yes, right-wing demagogues can hijack this struggle and pervert it into something to fear. But it is also our only hope for a future to believe in.

Eric Leif Davin, Ph.D., is the author of *The Great Strike of 1877; Crucible of Freedom: Workers' Democracy in the Industrial Heartland, 1914-1960; Radicals in Power: The New Left Experience in Office*; and, with Staughton Lynd, *Picket Line and Ballot Box: The Forgotten Legacy of the Labor Party Movement, 1932-1936*. He is also the author of *The Paterson Strike Pageant: An IWW Novel of Bohemia and Insurgent Labor* and *The Year of Hope and Fear: Insurrection and Repression, 1919*.

His essay, "The Very Last Hurrah: The Defeat of the Labor Party Idea, 1934-1936," appeared in *"We Are All Leaders: The Alternative Unionism of the Early 1930s,"* (University of Illinois Press, 1996), edited by Staughton Lynd. It won the Eugene V. Debs Foundation's prize as the best essay of that year reflecting the enduring spirit of Eugene V. Debs.

---

[i]. Carl Sandburg, "The People, Yes," in *The American Tradition in Literature*, Vol. 2, Edited by Sculley Bradley, Richmond Croom Beatty, and E. Hudson Long, W.W. Norton & Co.: New York, 1956, 960, 962.